50 Charcoal Grill Recipes

By: Kelly Johnson

Table of Contents

- Grilled Ribeye Steak
- Charcoal Grilled Chicken Thighs
- BBQ Pork Ribs
- Grilled Corn on the Cob
- Charcoal-Grilled Burgers
- Smoked Brisket
- Grilled Portobello Mushrooms
- Grilled Pineapple Slices
- Charcoal-Grilled Hot Dogs
- BBQ Chicken Wings
- Grilled Lamb Chops
- Grilled Zucchini and Squash
- Grilled Shrimp Skewers
- Smoked Sausage Links
- Grilled T-Bone Steak
- Charcoal-Grilled Salmon Fillets
- Grilled Vegetable Kabobs

- Smoked Pulled Pork
- Grilled Jalapeño Poppers
- Charcoal-Grilled Pizza
- Cedar Plank Salmon
- Grilled Eggplant Slices
- Charcoal BBQ Chicken Drumsticks
- Grilled Asparagus Bundles
- Charcoal-Smoked Turkey Breast
- Grilled Peaches with Honey
- Grilled Flat Iron Steak
- Grilled Cheese-Stuffed Burgers
- Grilled Chicken Kebabs
- Smoked Pork Tenderloin
- Charcoal-Grilled Lobster Tails
- Grilled Garlic Bread
- Grilled Halloumi Cheese
- Smoked Beef Ribs
- Grilled BBQ Meatballs
- Grilled Romaine Caesar Salad

- Charcoal-Grilled Tuna Steaks
- Smoked Mac and Cheese
- Grilled Bacon-Wrapped Scallops
- Grilled Chicken Fajitas
- Charcoal-Grilled Bratwurst
- Smoked Stuffed Bell Peppers
- Grilled Pineapple Chicken
- Grilled Steak Tacos
- BBQ Glazed Chicken Breasts
- Charcoal-Roasted Potatoes
- Grilled Pork Chops
- Smoked Chicken Wings
- Grilled Onion Slices
- Grilled BBQ Tofu

Grilled Ribeye Steak

Ingredients:

- 2 ribeye steaks (1-inch thick)
- Salt and pepper
- 2 tbsp olive oil
- 2 cloves garlic, minced
- 1 tbsp rosemary, chopped (optional)

Instructions:

1. Preheat grill to medium-high heat.
2. Season the steaks with salt, pepper, olive oil, garlic, and rosemary.
3. Grill for 4–5 minutes per side for medium-rare (adjust for desired doneness).
4. Let rest for 5 minutes before serving.

Charcoal Grilled Chicken Thighs

Ingredients:

- 4 bone-in, skin-on chicken thighs
- 1/4 cup olive oil
- 2 tbsp lemon juice
- 2 cloves garlic, minced
- 1 tbsp paprika
- Salt and pepper to taste

Instructions:

1. In a bowl, mix olive oil, lemon juice, garlic, paprika, salt, and pepper.
2. Coat chicken thighs with the marinade and refrigerate for at least 30 minutes.
3. Grill chicken on charcoal over medium heat, skin-side down, for 6–8 minutes per side.
4. Cook until internal temperature reaches 165°F.

BBQ Pork Ribs

Ingredients:

- 1 rack of baby back ribs
- 1/4 cup olive oil
- 1/4 cup apple cider vinegar
- 1/4 cup BBQ rub (store-bought or homemade)
- 1/2 cup BBQ sauce (for glazing)

Instructions:

1. Preheat grill for indirect cooking (low heat).
2. Rub ribs with olive oil, vinegar, and BBQ rub.
3. Place ribs on grill away from direct heat, cooking for 2–2.5 hours, turning occasionally.
4. During the last 15 minutes, glaze with BBQ sauce.
5. Let rest before slicing.

Grilled Corn on the Cob

Ingredients:

- 4 ears of corn, husked
- 2 tbsp butter
- Salt and pepper

Instructions:

1. Preheat the grill to medium heat.
2. Brush corn with melted butter, and season with salt and pepper.
3. Grill corn for 10–15 minutes, turning occasionally until charred and tender.
4. Serve with extra butter.

Charcoal-Grilled Burgers

Ingredients:

- 1 lb ground beef (80/20)
- Salt and pepper
- 4 burger buns
- Cheese slices (optional)
- Toppings: lettuce, tomato, pickles, onions

Instructions:

1. Form beef into 4 patties and season with salt and pepper.
2. Preheat grill to medium-high heat.
3. Grill burgers for 4–5 minutes per side or until desired doneness.
4. Toast buns and assemble with cheese and desired toppings.

Smoked Brisket

Ingredients:

- 1 whole brisket (5–7 lbs)
- 1/4 cup BBQ rub (store-bought or homemade)
- 1/4 cup apple cider vinegar
- 1/4 cup beef broth

Instructions:

1. Preheat smoker to 225°F.
2. Rub brisket with BBQ rub and let sit for 30 minutes.
3. Smoke brisket for 6–8 hours, spritzing with apple cider vinegar and beef broth every 2 hours.
4. When internal temperature reaches 195°F, remove and let rest for 20 minutes before slicing.

Grilled Portobello Mushrooms

Ingredients:

- 4 large portobello mushrooms, stems removed
- 2 tbsp olive oil
- 1 tbsp balsamic vinegar
- 2 cloves garlic, minced
- Salt and pepper

Instructions:

1. Mix olive oil, balsamic vinegar, garlic, salt, and pepper.
2. Brush mushrooms with the mixture.
3. Grill for 4–5 minutes per side until tender.
4. Serve as a side or on a bun for a vegetarian burger.

Grilled Pineapple Slices

Ingredients:

- 1 fresh pineapple, peeled and cut into 1/2-inch thick slices
- 1 tbsp honey (optional)
- 1 tsp cinnamon (optional)

Instructions:

1. Preheat grill to medium-high heat.
2. Brush pineapple slices with honey and sprinkle with cinnamon (if using).
3. Grill for 3–4 minutes per side until caramelized and grill marks appear.
4. Serve as a side or dessert.

Charcoal-Grilled Hot Dogs

Ingredients:

- 8 hot dog sausages
- 8 hot dog buns
- Ketchup, mustard, onions, relish (optional)

Instructions:

1. Preheat charcoal grill to medium-high heat.
2. Grill hot dogs for 5–7 minutes, turning occasionally until evenly charred.
3. Toast buns on the grill for the last minute of cooking.
4. Serve with your favorite toppings.

BBQ Chicken Wings

Ingredients:

- 12 chicken wings
- 1/4 cup BBQ sauce
- 1 tbsp olive oil
- Salt and pepper to taste
- 1 tsp garlic powder

Instructions:

1. Preheat grill to medium heat.
2. Toss wings in olive oil, salt, pepper, and garlic powder.
3. Grill wings for 8–10 minutes per side, until crispy and cooked through.
4. Brush with BBQ sauce during the last 5 minutes of grilling.
5. Serve hot with extra BBQ sauce on the side.

Grilled Lamb Chops

Ingredients:

- 8 lamb chops
- 2 tbsp olive oil
- 2 cloves garlic, minced
- 1 tbsp rosemary, chopped
- Salt and pepper to taste

Instructions:

1. Preheat grill to medium-high heat.
2. Rub lamb chops with olive oil, garlic, rosemary, salt, and pepper.
3. Grill chops for 4–5 minutes per side for medium-rare, adjusting for desired doneness.
4. Let rest for 5 minutes before serving.

Grilled Zucchini and Squash

Ingredients:

- 2 zucchinis, sliced
- 2 yellow squashes, sliced
- 2 tbsp olive oil
- Salt and pepper to taste
- 1 tsp Italian seasoning

Instructions:

1. Preheat grill to medium heat.
2. Toss zucchini and squash slices with olive oil, salt, pepper, and Italian seasoning.
3. Grill for 3–4 minutes per side until tender and slightly charred.
4. Serve as a side dish or top with parmesan cheese.

Grilled Shrimp Skewers

Ingredients:

- 1 lb shrimp, peeled and deveined
- 2 tbsp olive oil
- 2 tbsp lemon juice
- 2 cloves garlic, minced
- Salt and pepper to taste
- 1 tsp paprika

Instructions:

1. Preheat grill to medium-high heat.
2. Toss shrimp in olive oil, lemon juice, garlic, salt, pepper, and paprika.
3. Thread shrimp onto skewers.
4. Grill for 2–3 minutes per side, until shrimp are opaque.
5. Serve with lemon wedges and a side of dipping sauce.

Smoked Sausage Links

Ingredients:

- 4 smoked sausage links
- 1 tbsp olive oil
- 1 tsp garlic powder
- 1 tsp paprika
- Salt and pepper to taste

Instructions:

1. Preheat grill to medium heat.
2. Rub sausage links with olive oil, garlic powder, paprika, salt, and pepper.
3. Grill sausages for 5–7 minutes per side until golden and crispy.
4. Serve on buns with mustard or your favorite toppings.

Grilled T-Bone Steak

Ingredients:

- 2 T-bone steaks
- Salt and pepper to taste
- 2 tbsp olive oil
- 2 cloves garlic, minced
- 1 tbsp rosemary, chopped (optional)

Instructions:

1. Preheat grill to high heat.
2. Rub steaks with olive oil, garlic, rosemary, salt, and pepper.
3. Grill steaks for 4–5 minutes per side for medium-rare, adjusting for desired doneness.
4. Let rest for 5 minutes before serving.

Charcoal-Grilled Salmon Fillets

Ingredients:

- 2 salmon fillets
- 2 tbsp olive oil
- 1 tbsp lemon juice
- Salt and pepper to taste
- 1 tsp dill (optional)

Instructions:

1. Preheat charcoal grill to medium heat.
2. Brush salmon fillets with olive oil, lemon juice, salt, pepper, and dill.
3. Grill skin-side down for 4–5 minutes, then flip and grill for another 3–4 minutes.
4. Serve with lemon wedges.

Grilled Vegetable Kabobs

Ingredients:

- 1 bell pepper, chopped
- 1 zucchini, chopped
- 1 red onion, chopped
- 1 cup mushrooms, whole
- 2 tbsp olive oil
- Salt and pepper to taste
- 1 tsp Italian seasoning

Instructions:

1. Preheat grill to medium heat.
2. Skewer the vegetables onto wooden or metal skewers.
3. Brush with olive oil and season with salt, pepper, and Italian seasoning.
4. Grill kabobs for 4–5 minutes per side, until vegetables are tender and slightly charred.
5. Serve as a side dish or over rice.

Smoked Pulled Pork

Ingredients:

- 4–5 lb pork shoulder
- 2 tbsp olive oil
- 1/4 cup BBQ rub
- 1/4 cup apple cider vinegar
- 1/4 cup BBQ sauce

Instructions:

1. Preheat smoker to 225°F.
2. Rub the pork shoulder with olive oil and BBQ rub.
3. Smoke for 8–10 hours, basting with apple cider vinegar every few hours.
4. Once internal temperature reaches 190°F, remove and let rest for 20 minutes.
5. Shred the pork using forks and toss with BBQ sauce. Serve on buns.

Grilled Jalapeño Poppers

Ingredients:

- 12 jalapeños, halved and seeded
- 8 oz cream cheese, softened
- 1/2 cup shredded cheddar cheese
- 1/4 cup cooked bacon, crumbled
- Salt and pepper to taste
- 12 slices bacon (optional)

Instructions:

1. Preheat grill to medium heat.
2. Mix cream cheese, cheddar cheese, crumbled bacon, salt, and pepper in a bowl.
3. Stuff the jalapeño halves with the cheese mixture.
4. If using, wrap each stuffed jalapeño with a slice of bacon.
5. Grill for 8–10 minutes, turning occasionally, until the peppers are softened and the bacon is crispy.
6. Serve hot with a drizzle of BBQ sauce if desired.

Charcoal-Grilled Pizza

Ingredients:

- 1 pizza dough (store-bought or homemade)
- 1/2 cup tomato sauce
- 1 1/2 cups shredded mozzarella cheese
- Toppings of choice (e.g., pepperoni, vegetables, olives, etc.)
- Olive oil for brushing

Instructions:

1. Preheat charcoal grill to medium-high heat.
2. Roll out the pizza dough on a floured surface to your desired size.
3. Brush the dough lightly with olive oil on both sides.
4. Place the dough on the grill for 2–3 minutes until lightly charred.
5. Flip the dough, spread tomato sauce, sprinkle mozzarella, and add toppings.
6. Close the grill lid and cook for another 4–6 minutes until cheese is melted and crust is golden.
7. Slice and serve immediately.

Cedar Plank Salmon

Ingredients:

- 2 salmon fillets
- 1 cedar plank (soaked in water for at least 30 minutes)
- 2 tbsp olive oil
- 1 tbsp lemon juice
- Salt and pepper to taste
- 1 tsp dill or rosemary (optional)

Instructions:

1. Preheat grill to medium heat.
2. Brush the salmon fillets with olive oil and lemon juice. Season with salt, pepper, and dill or rosemary.
3. Place the cedar plank on the grill for 2–3 minutes to heat it up.
4. Place the salmon fillets skin-side down on the plank.
5. Grill for 12–15 minutes, until the salmon is cooked through.
6. Serve directly from the plank for a rustic presentation.

Grilled Eggplant Slices

Ingredients:

- 2 eggplants, sliced into 1/2-inch rounds
- 3 tbsp olive oil
- 1 tsp garlic powder
- Salt and pepper to taste
- 1 tbsp balsamic vinegar (optional)

Instructions:

1. Preheat grill to medium-high heat.
2. Brush the eggplant slices with olive oil, garlic powder, salt, and pepper.
3. Grill the slices for 4–5 minutes per side, until tender and charred.
4. Drizzle with balsamic vinegar before serving for added flavor.

Charcoal BBQ Chicken Drumsticks

Ingredients:

- 10 chicken drumsticks
- 1/4 cup BBQ sauce
- 1 tbsp olive oil
- Salt and pepper to taste
- 1 tsp paprika

Instructions:

1. Preheat charcoal grill to medium heat.
2. Rub chicken drumsticks with olive oil, salt, pepper, and paprika.
3. Grill the drumsticks for 25–30 minutes, turning every 5–7 minutes.
4. Brush with BBQ sauce during the last 10 minutes of grilling.
5. Serve with extra BBQ sauce on the side.

Grilled Asparagus Bundles

Ingredients:

- 1 bunch asparagus, trimmed
- 4 slices prosciutto or bacon (optional)
- 1 tbsp olive oil
- Salt and pepper to taste
- 1 tbsp lemon juice (optional)

Instructions:

1. Preheat grill to medium heat.
2. Arrange asparagus into bundles of 4–5 spears and wrap with prosciutto or bacon if desired.
3. Brush with olive oil and season with salt and pepper.
4. Grill bundles for 4–5 minutes per side, until tender and slightly charred.
5. Drizzle with lemon juice before serving for added freshness.

Charcoal-Smoked Turkey Breast

Ingredients:

- 3–4 lb turkey breast, bone-in or boneless
- 1/4 cup olive oil
- 2 tbsp paprika
- 1 tbsp garlic powder
- Salt and pepper to taste
- Wood chips for smoking

Instructions:

1. Preheat charcoal grill to low heat (around 225°F) and add wood chips for smoke.
2. Rub turkey breast with olive oil, paprika, garlic powder, salt, and pepper.
3. Place turkey breast on the grill away from direct heat, cover, and smoke for 2–3 hours, or until internal temperature reaches 165°F.
4. Let rest for 10 minutes before slicing. Serve with cranberry sauce or gravy.

Grilled Peaches with Honey

Ingredients:

- 4 peaches, halved and pitted
- 2 tbsp honey
- 1 tbsp olive oil
- 1/2 tsp cinnamon (optional)

Instructions:

1. Preheat grill to medium heat.
2. Brush peach halves with olive oil.
3. Grill peaches cut-side down for 4–5 minutes until grill marks form and peaches are tender.
4. Drizzle with honey and sprinkle with cinnamon if desired before serving.

Grilled Flat Iron Steak

Ingredients:

- 2 flat iron steaks
- 2 tbsp olive oil
- 1 tbsp balsamic vinegar
- Salt and pepper to taste
- 2 cloves garlic, minced
- 1 tbsp rosemary, chopped (optional)

Instructions:

1. Preheat grill to high heat.
2. Rub steaks with olive oil, balsamic vinegar, garlic, rosemary, salt, and pepper.
3. Grill steaks for 4–5 minutes per side for medium-rare, adjusting for your preferred doneness.
4. Let rest for 5 minutes before slicing against the grain and serving.

Grilled Cheese-Stuffed Burgers

Ingredients:

- 1 lb ground beef (80/20 blend)
- 4 oz cheddar cheese, cut into small cubes
- 1 tbsp Worcestershire sauce
- 1 tsp garlic powder
- Salt and pepper to taste
- Burger buns

Instructions:

1. Preheat grill to medium-high heat.
2. Form the ground beef into 8 small patties. Place a cube of cheese in the center of 4 patties. Top with the remaining patties and seal the edges.
3. Season the burgers with Worcestershire sauce, garlic powder, salt, and pepper.
4. Grill the burgers for 4–5 minutes per side, or until cooked to your desired doneness.
5. Toast the buns on the grill during the last minute of cooking.
6. Assemble the burgers on the buns and serve.

Grilled Chicken Kebabs

Ingredients:

- 2 chicken breasts, cut into 1-inch cubes
- 1 red bell pepper, cut into 1-inch pieces
- 1 zucchini, sliced
- 1 onion, cut into wedges
- 1/4 cup olive oil
- 2 tbsp soy sauce
- 1 tbsp lemon juice
- 1 tsp garlic powder
- 1 tsp paprika
- Salt and pepper to taste

Instructions:

1. Preheat grill to medium-high heat.
2. In a bowl, mix olive oil, soy sauce, lemon juice, garlic powder, paprika, salt, and pepper.
3. Thread the chicken, bell pepper, zucchini, and onion onto skewers, alternating ingredients.
4. Brush the kebabs with the marinade.
5. Grill the kebabs for 8–10 minutes, turning occasionally, until the chicken is cooked through.

6. Serve immediately with your favorite dipping sauce or side.

Smoked Pork Tenderloin

Ingredients:

- 2 pork tenderloins (about 1 lb each)
- 2 tbsp olive oil
- 1 tbsp brown sugar
- 1 tbsp smoked paprika
- 1 tsp garlic powder
- 1 tsp onion powder
- Salt and pepper to taste
- Wood chips for smoking

Instructions:

1. Preheat grill to low heat (225°F) and prepare the smoker with wood chips.
2. Rub the pork tenderloins with olive oil and then coat with brown sugar, smoked paprika, garlic powder, onion powder, salt, and pepper.
3. Place the pork tenderloins on the grill, away from direct heat. Close the lid and smoke for 2–3 hours, or until the internal temperature reaches 145°F.
4. Let the tenderloins rest for 10 minutes before slicing and serving.

Charcoal-Grilled Lobster Tails

Ingredients:

- 4 lobster tails
- 1/4 cup butter, melted
- 2 cloves garlic, minced
- 1 tbsp lemon juice
- Salt and pepper to taste
- 1 tbsp chopped parsley (optional)

Instructions:

1. Preheat charcoal grill to medium-high heat.
2. Use kitchen shears to cut the lobster tails in half lengthwise.
3. In a small bowl, mix melted butter, garlic, lemon juice, salt, and pepper.
4. Brush the lobster meat with the butter mixture.
5. Grill the lobster tails meat-side down for 5–7 minutes, then flip and grill for another 3–5 minutes, until the lobster meat is opaque and cooked through.
6. Garnish with parsley and serve with additional lemon wedges.

Grilled Garlic Bread

Ingredients:

- 1 baguette or Italian loaf, sliced in half lengthwise
- 1/4 cup butter, softened
- 3 cloves garlic, minced
- 1 tbsp fresh parsley, chopped
- Salt to taste

Instructions:

1. Preheat grill to medium heat.
2. In a bowl, mix softened butter, minced garlic, parsley, and salt.
3. Spread the garlic butter mixture on the cut sides of the bread.
4. Place the bread on the grill, buttered-side down, and grill for 2–3 minutes, until the bread is toasted and golden.
5. Serve warm with your favorite pasta or BBQ dish.

Grilled Halloumi Cheese

Ingredients:

- 8 oz halloumi cheese, sliced into 1/2-inch thick slices
- 1 tbsp olive oil
- 1 tbsp lemon juice
- Fresh mint for garnish (optional)

Instructions:

1. Preheat grill to medium-high heat.
2. Brush the halloumi slices with olive oil.
3. Grill the cheese for 2–3 minutes per side, until golden brown and grill marks appear.
4. Drizzle with lemon juice and garnish with fresh mint before serving.

Smoked Beef Ribs

Ingredients:

- 2 racks of beef ribs
- 1/4 cup olive oil
- 2 tbsp brown sugar
- 1 tbsp smoked paprika
- 1 tsp garlic powder
- Salt and pepper to taste
- Wood chips for smoking

Instructions:

1. Preheat grill to low heat (around 225°F) and prepare the smoker with wood chips.
2. Rub the ribs with olive oil, brown sugar, smoked paprika, garlic powder, salt, and pepper.
3. Place the ribs on the grill, away from direct heat. Close the lid and smoke for 4–5 hours, until the ribs are tender and the meat pulls away from the bone.
4. Serve with your favorite BBQ sauce.

Grilled BBQ Meatballs

Ingredients:

- 1 lb ground beef or pork
- 1/4 cup breadcrumbs
- 1/4 cup grated Parmesan cheese
- 1 egg
- 1 tbsp garlic powder
- 1 tbsp onion powder
- 1/2 tsp dried oregano
- Salt and pepper to taste
- 1/2 cup BBQ sauce

Instructions:

1. Preheat grill to medium-high heat.
2. In a bowl, combine ground meat, breadcrumbs, Parmesan, egg, garlic powder, onion powder, oregano, salt, and pepper. Mix well and form into small meatballs.
3. Grill the meatballs for 8–10 minutes, turning occasionally, until cooked through.
4. Brush with BBQ sauce during the last 2 minutes of grilling.
5. Serve hot with extra BBQ sauce on the side.

Grilled Romaine Caesar Salad

Ingredients:

- 2 heads romaine lettuce, halved
- 2 tbsp olive oil
- Salt and pepper to taste
- 1/2 cup Caesar dressing
- 1/4 cup grated Parmesan cheese
- Croutons for garnish

Instructions:

1. Preheat grill to medium heat.
2. Brush the cut sides of the romaine halves with olive oil and season with salt and pepper.
3. Grill the romaine halves for 2–3 minutes, cut-side down, until lightly charred.
4. Drizzle with Caesar dressing, sprinkle with Parmesan cheese, and garnish with croutons. Serve immediately.

Charcoal-Grilled Tuna Steaks

Ingredients:

- 4 tuna steaks (about 1-inch thick)
- 2 tbsp olive oil
- 2 tbsp soy sauce
- 1 tbsp lemon juice
- 1 tsp garlic powder
- 1 tsp onion powder
- Salt and pepper to taste

Instructions:

1. Preheat grill to medium-high heat.
2. In a bowl, mix olive oil, soy sauce, lemon juice, garlic powder, onion powder, salt, and pepper.
3. Brush the tuna steaks with the marinade.
4. Grill the tuna steaks for 3–4 minutes per side for medium-rare, or longer if desired.
5. Serve immediately with a squeeze of lemon.

Smoked Mac and Cheese

Ingredients:

- 1 lb elbow macaroni
- 4 tbsp butter
- 2 tbsp flour
- 3 cups whole milk
- 2 cups shredded cheddar cheese
- 1 cup shredded mozzarella cheese
- 1/2 cup grated Parmesan cheese
- Salt and pepper to taste
- 1/2 tsp smoked paprika
- 1/2 cup breadcrumbs (optional)

Instructions:

1. Preheat smoker to 225°F.
2. Cook macaroni according to package directions, drain, and set aside.
3. In a saucepan, melt butter over medium heat. Stir in flour and cook for 1 minute.
4. Gradually add milk, whisking constantly until thickened. Stir in the cheddar, mozzarella, and Parmesan cheese until melted and smooth.
5. Add the cooked macaroni, smoked paprika, salt, and pepper, and mix well.
6. Pour the mac and cheese into a baking dish and top with breadcrumbs if desired.

7. Smoke for 45 minutes to 1 hour, stirring halfway through. Serve warm.

Grilled Bacon-Wrapped Scallops

Ingredients:

- 12 large scallops
- 12 slices bacon
- 1 tbsp olive oil
- 1 tsp garlic powder
- 1 tsp smoked paprika
- Salt and pepper to taste
- Lemon wedges for serving

Instructions:

1. Preheat grill to medium-high heat.
2. Wrap each scallop with a slice of bacon and secure with a toothpick.
3. Drizzle with olive oil and season with garlic powder, smoked paprika, salt, and pepper.
4. Grill the scallops for 2–3 minutes per side, or until the bacon is crispy and the scallops are cooked through.
5. Serve with lemon wedges.

Grilled Chicken Fajitas

Ingredients:

- 4 boneless, skinless chicken breasts
- 2 tbsp olive oil
- 1 tbsp lime juice
- 1 tsp chili powder
- 1 tsp cumin
- 1 tsp garlic powder
- Salt and pepper to taste
- 1 red bell pepper, sliced
- 1 yellow bell pepper, sliced
- 1 onion, sliced
- Flour tortillas for serving
- Fresh cilantro and lime wedges for garnish

Instructions:

1. Preheat grill to medium-high heat.
2. In a bowl, combine olive oil, lime juice, chili powder, cumin, garlic powder, salt, and pepper.
3. Coat the chicken breasts with the marinade and let them sit for 10-15 minutes.
4. Grill the chicken for 6–7 minutes per side, or until fully cooked.

5. Grill the bell peppers and onion for 3–4 minutes, or until tender and charred.

6. Slice the chicken and serve with the grilled vegetables on tortillas. Garnish with fresh cilantro and lime wedges.

Charcoal-Grilled Bratwurst

Ingredients:

- 4 bratwurst sausages
- 1 tbsp olive oil
- 1/2 cup beer (optional)
- 1 onion, sliced
- Mustard and sauerkraut for serving

Instructions:

1. Preheat grill to medium heat.
2. Brush the bratwurst with olive oil and place them on the grill.
3. Grill the bratwurst for 6–8 minutes per side, or until they reach an internal temperature of 160°F.
4. While grilling, sauté the onions in a skillet over medium heat with a bit of oil until caramelized, about 5–7 minutes.
5. Serve the bratwurst with the sautéed onions, mustard, and sauerkraut.

Smoked Stuffed Bell Peppers

Ingredients:

- 4 bell peppers, tops cut off and seeds removed
- 1 lb ground beef or turkey
- 1 cup cooked rice
- 1/2 cup shredded cheese (cheddar, mozzarella, or a mix)
- 1 can diced tomatoes
- 1 tsp garlic powder
- 1 tsp onion powder
- Salt and pepper to taste
- 1 tbsp olive oil

Instructions:

1. Preheat smoker to 225°F.
2. In a skillet, brown the ground meat and season with garlic powder, onion powder, salt, and pepper.
3. Stir in the cooked rice, diced tomatoes, and half of the cheese.
4. Stuff the bell peppers with the meat and rice mixture.
5. Drizzle with olive oil and smoke the stuffed peppers for 45 minutes to 1 hour, until the peppers are tender.
6. Top with the remaining cheese and smoke for an additional 5 minutes to melt the cheese. Serve hot.

Grilled Pineapple Chicken

Ingredients:

- 4 boneless, skinless chicken breasts
- 1 fresh pineapple, peeled, cored, and cut into rings
- 1/4 cup soy sauce
- 1/4 cup honey
- 2 tbsp lime juice
- 2 tbsp olive oil
- 1 tsp garlic powder
- Salt and pepper to taste

Instructions:

1. Preheat grill to medium heat.
2. In a bowl, combine soy sauce, honey, lime juice, olive oil, garlic powder, salt, and pepper.
3. Marinate the chicken breasts in the mixture for at least 30 minutes.
4. Grill the chicken for 6–7 minutes per side, or until fully cooked.
5. Grill the pineapple rings for 2–3 minutes per side until caramelized.
6. Serve the grilled chicken with the pineapple rings on top.

Grilled Steak Tacos

Ingredients:

- 2 flank steaks (about 1 lb each)
- 1 tbsp olive oil
- 1 tbsp lime juice
- 1 tsp chili powder
- 1 tsp cumin
- 1 tsp garlic powder
- Salt and pepper to taste
- Flour tortillas for serving
- Fresh cilantro, onion, and lime wedges for garnish

Instructions:

1. Preheat grill to medium-high heat.
2. In a bowl, mix olive oil, lime juice, chili powder, cumin, garlic powder, salt, and pepper.
3. Coat the flank steaks with the marinade and let them sit for 10-15 minutes.
4. Grill the steaks for 4–5 minutes per side for medium-rare, or longer if desired.
5. Let the steaks rest for 5 minutes before slicing thinly.
6. Serve the steak slices on tortillas with fresh cilantro, onion, and lime wedges.

BBQ Glazed Chicken Breasts

Ingredients:

- 4 boneless, skinless chicken breasts
- 1/2 cup BBQ sauce (your favorite brand)
- 1 tbsp olive oil
- Salt and pepper to taste

Instructions:

1. Preheat grill to medium heat.
2. Brush the chicken breasts with olive oil and season with salt and pepper.
3. Grill the chicken for 6–7 minutes per side, until fully cooked (internal temperature should reach 165°F).
4. During the last 2 minutes of grilling, brush the chicken with BBQ sauce and grill until caramelized.
5. Serve the BBQ chicken with additional sauce on the side.

Charcoal-Roasted Potatoes

Ingredients:

- 4 large potatoes, cut into wedges
- 2 tbsp olive oil
- 1 tsp garlic powder
- 1 tsp smoked paprika
- Salt and pepper to taste
- Fresh parsley for garnish

Instructions:

1. Preheat the grill to medium-high heat.
2. In a bowl, toss the potato wedges with olive oil, garlic powder, smoked paprika, salt, and pepper.
3. Wrap the seasoned potatoes in foil, creating a tightly sealed packet.
4. Place the foil packet on the grill over indirect heat and cook for 35–40 minutes, turning halfway through.
5. Once tender, remove from the grill, garnish with fresh parsley, and serve.

Grilled Pork Chops

Ingredients:

- 4 bone-in pork chops (about 1-inch thick)
- 2 tbsp olive oil
- 1 tbsp brown sugar
- 1 tbsp Dijon mustard
- 1 tsp garlic powder
- 1 tsp smoked paprika
- Salt and pepper to taste

Instructions:

1. Preheat the grill to medium-high heat.
2. In a bowl, combine olive oil, brown sugar, Dijon mustard, garlic powder, smoked paprika, salt, and pepper.
3. Brush the pork chops with the marinade and let them sit for 10 minutes.
4. Grill the pork chops for 5–7 minutes per side, or until they reach an internal temperature of 145°F.
5. Let the chops rest for 5 minutes before serving.

Smoked Chicken Wings

Ingredients:

- 12 chicken wings
- 2 tbsp olive oil
- 1 tbsp paprika
- 1 tsp garlic powder
- 1 tsp onion powder
- 1 tsp chili powder
- Salt and pepper to taste
- 1/2 cup BBQ sauce (optional)

Instructions:

1. Preheat your smoker to 225°F.
2. In a bowl, mix olive oil, paprika, garlic powder, onion powder, chili powder, salt, and pepper.
3. Toss the chicken wings with the seasoning mixture and let them sit for 10 minutes.
4. Place the wings on the smoker and cook for 2–2.5 hours, or until the internal temperature reaches 165°F.
5. Optional: During the last 10 minutes, brush the wings with BBQ sauce.
6. Serve hot.

Grilled Onion Slices

Ingredients:

- 2 large onions, peeled and cut into 1-inch thick slices
- 2 tbsp olive oil
- 1 tsp garlic powder
- 1 tsp balsamic vinegar
- Salt and pepper to taste
- Fresh herbs (optional, for garnish)

Instructions:

1. Preheat the grill to medium heat.
2. Brush the onion slices with olive oil and balsamic vinegar, and season with garlic powder, salt, and pepper.
3. Grill the onion slices for 3–4 minutes per side, or until tender and charred.
4. Remove from the grill, garnish with fresh herbs if desired, and serve.

Grilled BBQ Tofu

Ingredients:

- 1 block firm tofu, pressed and cut into 1-inch thick slices
- 1/2 cup BBQ sauce
- 1 tbsp olive oil
- Salt and pepper to taste

Instructions:

1. Preheat the grill to medium heat.
2. Brush the tofu slices with olive oil and season with salt and pepper.
3. Grill the tofu slices for 3–4 minutes per side, or until crispy and charred.
4. Brush the tofu with BBQ sauce during the last 2 minutes of grilling.
5. Serve hot, with additional BBQ sauce on the side if desired.

www.ingramcontent.com/pod-product-compliance
Lightning Source LLC
LaVergne TN
LVHW081321060526
838201LV00055B/2397